CAPYBARA For Kids

Fun Facts, photos & Fascinating info about the world's largest rodent.

Published by
GRAPEVINE BOOKS

www.grapevinebooks.com
email: contact@grapevinebooks.com
Ordering Information:
Quantity sales: Special discounts are available on quantity purchases
by corporations, associations, and others.
For details, reach out to the publisher.

First published by Grapevine Books 2025

TABLE Of CONTENTS

Hello there, friend! I'm Cappy the Capybara, and I'm so excited you're here!

I may look like a giant guinea pig (that's my cousin, by the way), but I'm actually the **biggest rodent** in the whole wide world. I live in the warm, splashy lands of **South America** where I spend my days swimming, snacking, snoozing, and hanging out with my big group of capybara buddies.

Guess what? I'm not just cute. I'm full of cool secrets too! In this book, I'll take you on a journey through my world. You'll learn how I talk, what I eat, why I roll in mud, and who my wildest animal friends are (some may surprise you!).

So grab your explorer hat, open your eyes wide, and get ready for a capy-tastic adventure!
Let's go!

Your pal,
Cappy

Chapter 1: My Jungle Home

Welcome to the wild! I'm going to show you where I live and what makes it so special. My home isn't a house or a nest; it's a big, beautiful piece of nature. Ready to explore?

Let's go!

I live in **South America**, in places like Brazil, Colombia, and Venezuela.
You'll find me wherever there's lots of water.

My favorite homes are near **rivers, ponds, swamps, and lakes**. I'm never far from a splash!

I love spots with **tall grass, soft mud, and leafy plants**. They help me stay cool, fed, and hidden.

I share my neighborhood with animals like **frogs, turtles, monkeys, birds, and even crocodiles**!

I'm most active in the **early morning and late afternoon**, when it's not too hot.

During the warmest part of the day, I take long naps in the **shade or float in the water** with just my nose showing.

Pretty neat, right? Nature gave me the perfect home; muddy, leafy, splashy, and safe. Let's keep going!

Chapter 2: Big and Chill

I may look like a giant guinea pig (because I kind of am), but don't let my size fool you. I'm not wild or scary. I'm calm, friendly, and super chill. Let me show you what makes me such a relaxed and lovable giant.

I'm the **biggest rodent in the world**! I can grow up to 4 feet long and weigh as much as 150 pounds.

Even though I'm big, I'm not dangerous. I have **no sharp claws or scary teeth,** just a gentle mouth for munching plants.

My body is shaped like a **giant potato with legs**: round, low, and soft. Some people say I look like a walking loaf of bread!

I'm super **quiet and peaceful**. I don't bark or growl or make a fuss unless I really have to.

I spend a lot of my day just **sitting, chewing, or soaking in water**, kind of like an animal spa day, every day.

I don't fight. I don't chase. I **move slowly**, stay calm, and mind my own business. It works out pretty well!

So yeah, I'm big, but I'm also easygoing, quiet, and kind. Being chill is kind of my superpower. Want to meet my capybara crew next?

Chapter 3: My Capybara Family

I never live alone, and I wouldn't want to! I'm a capybara, and that means I'm part of a big, warm, fuzzy family. We eat together, nap together, and look out for each other.
Let me introduce you to herd life!

Capybaras live in herds, which are groups of 10-30 capybaras who stay together like a team.

We're always in contact; grooming, cuddling, or sitting close so we feel safe and connected.

When one capybara spots danger, they make a sharp barking sound to warn the whole group.

We take turns watching for predators while others nap or eat. Everyone helps keep the group safe.

Baby capybaras, called pups, are cared for by the whole herd, not just their mom!

We love to snuggle in big capy piles, especially when we're sleepy or cold. It's the best kind of group hug!

I'm never alone, and that's how I like it. We eat together, nap together, and move together like one big happy team.
Life just feels better when you've got your herd around you, watching your back and sharing the shade.

Chapter 4: Snack Time!

Let's talk about my favorite part of the day: mealtime! I eat a lot, and I mean A LOT. But I'm picky in the best way; I only eat plants. Want to see what's on the capybara menu? Let's dig in!

I'm a herbivore, which means I eat only plants. No meat, ever!

I munch on grass, leaves, fruit, and water plants all day long.

My teeth never stop growing, so I have to chew plants to keep them from getting too long!

Sometimes I eat my poop... yep!
It's called coprophagy and it helps me digest my food better the second time.

I don't eat fast. I like to graze slowly throughout the day, just like a cow.

Eating together is part of our routine. It helps our herd stay calm and connected while we fill our bellies.

I don't need fancy meals to be happy. Give me some fresh grass, maybe a crunchy leaf or two, and I'll be the happiest capy around. Nature gives me everything I need, one bite at a time.

Chapter 5: Capy Talk

We capybaras may not speak like humans, but we sure do talk! From squeaks to purrs to barks, we use lots of sounds to share how we feel. Want to learn our secret language? Listen closely!

When I'm happy, I make a gentle purring sound. Just like a cat!

I whistle when I'm excited or calling to my family.

When I sense danger, I bark: a loud, sharp "ARF!" to warn everyone around me.

I also click my teeth when I'm annoyed or want more space.

Baby capybaras squeak and whimper when they want attention from grown-ups.

We don't just make noise.
We use our sounds to stay safe and stay close to our herd.

I may not use words like you do, but I've got plenty to say! Each sound I make helps me stay connected to my herd. It's our way of saying, "I'm here, I'm safe, I hear you."

Chapter 6: Capy Pup Life

Believe it or not, I was once a teeny-tiny capybara pup! Capy babies are some of the cutest, cuddliest animals you'll ever see, and we grow up fast. Let me tell you what life was like when I was just starting out.

Capybara babies are called pups, and we're born with fur, teeth, and open eyes!

Within hours of being born, I could walk, run, and swim on my own.

I drank milk from my mom for about 3 months while learning to munch on grass.

In our herd, every adult helps take care of the pups, not just our moms.

We love to play! Pups chase each other, roll in the mud, and splash around all day.

At night, we snuggle close to the grown-ups: safe, warm, and sleepy.

When we're born, we're tiny but brave; ready to walk, swim, and squeak from the start! But we're never alone. Grown-up capys keep us warm, show us where to eat, and teach us how to stay safe. Every day is a new adventure, and every cuddle makes us stronger.

Chapter 7: Water Is My Happy Place

Some animals like climbing trees.
Others love digging tunnels. Me? I'm
happiest when I'm in the water!
Swimming, soaking, or just floating;
water is my favorite place to be.
Come take a dip with me!

I'm a great swimmer with webbed feet
that help me paddle fast.

I can hold my breath for up to 5 minutes
underwater; long enough to hide from predators!

Sometimes I sleep in the water, with just my nose
sticking out to breathe.

When the weather's hot, I cool off by floating or diving into rivers and ponds.

My eyes, ears, and nose are on top of my head, so I can stay mostly underwater but still see and hear.

Water keeps me safe, cool, and calm. It's like my very own capybara bathtub!

Water is where I feel most at peace. Whether I'm diving deep, floating still, or napping with just my nose in the air, the river is my quiet friend. It cools me down, keeps me safe, and lets me drift away without a care.

Chapter 8: Capybara Spa Day

Forget fancy spas. I've got mud! It cools me down, protects my skin, and keeps the bugs away. Rolling in mud might sound messy, but for a capybara, it's the secret to looking and feeling our best.

I roll in mud to stay cool on hot days. Mud works like natural sunscreen!

A thick coat of mud keeps away mosquitoes and biting bugs.

Mud helps me regulate my body temperature, especially when there's no shade.

We love sitting in puddles together. Mud baths are a group activity in capy life!

After a good soak, I often head straight to the water to rinse off and relax.

It may look messy, but mud keeps my skin healthy, protected, and happy.

Some animals go to fancy spas, but me? I roll in mud, soak in puddles, and let the earth do the rest. Mud cools me down, keeps bugs away, and makes my skin feel just right. It may look messy, but to a capybara, a muddy splash is pure joy. It's nature's spa, and I never miss a day!

Chapter 9: My Animal Buddies

I'm not just friendly with my capybara family, I get along with almost everyone! Birds, turtles, monkeys, even cats and dogs. Animals like hanging out with me because I stay calm and make space for everyone. Let me introduce you to some of my pals!

Birds love sitting on my back; they feel safe, and sometimes they even help pick off bugs!

I'm known to chill near turtles, ducks, and deer, and nobody gets scared.

Some monkeys swing in the trees above me, and we just hang out, doing our own thing.

In zoos and farms, dogs, cats, rabbits, and goats sometimes share space with me.

Because I don't bark, chase, or fight, other animals feel relaxed around me.

People around the world call me "the friendliest animal on Earth."

I don't need to bark or chase or show off to make friends. I just stay calm, share my space, and let others come as they are. That's why turtles nap beside me, birds perch on my back, and monkeys swing nearby without fear. In the jungle, peace makes the best kind of friendship.

Chapter 10: Fast Capy Facts!

Let's zip through some of my all-time favorite capybara facts! These are the kind of facts that make people say, "Wait... what?!" Get ready for some weird, wild, and wonderful surprises.

I'm related to guinea pigs. They're my tiny cousins!

I have no tail, but super strong back legs for swimming and waddling.

My teeth never stop growing, so I have to chew plants to keep them in check.

I sometimes eat my poop (yep, again!). It helps me absorb extra nutrients.

I can sleep with my nose sticking out of water, like a mini submarine.

People think I look like a walking potato or coconut; and honestly, I don't mind!

Whew! That was a lot of facts, right? But that's just the thing about capybaras: we look simple, but we're full of surprises. From my teeth to my toes to my potato-shaped body, every part of me tells a story. And the more you learn, the more there is to love.

Chapter 11: A Day in My Capy Life

Ever wonder what I do all day? Spoiler: it's a mix of snacks, naps, and splashes! Capybaras like me follow the rhythm of nature. Let me walk you through my perfect, peaceful capy day.

I wake up early in the morning, when the sun is just rising and the air feels fresh.

First things first, I graze on grass or water plants to start the day with a full belly.

After breakfast, I take a swim to cool down and stretch my legs.

When the sun gets hot, I find shade or float in water to relax and nap.

In the late afternoon, I wake up, eat again, and enjoy the cooler air.

At night, I settle down with my herd and sleep close to my family, safe and warm.

My days aren't loud or rushed. They follow the sun and the breeze. I eat when I'm hungry, swim when I'm warm, and rest when I'm full. Life is slow, simple, and peaceful, just the way I like it. Every capy day is a calm adventure waiting to unfold.

Chapter 12: Capybara Habitats Around the World

Even though capybaras are wild animals, you can find us in all kinds of places: from big rivers to small city zoos. Let me show you where we live, roam, and splash across the globe!

Capybaras are native to South America, especially countries like Brazil, Colombia, Venezuela, and Argentina.

We live near rivers, lakes, swamps, and wetlands; anywhere with fresh water and plants.

Capybaras are also found in flooded forests and grassy plains, where the ground stays soft and damp.

In some places, we even live near farms or towns, especially if there's a stream or canal nearby.

You can visit capybaras at zoos and wildlife parks all over the world, from Japan to the U.S.!

In warm countries like Panama and Paraguay, we're a common sight lounging by rivers and walking through grass

From the wetlands of Brazil to city parks and quiet zoo corners, capybaras have found homes all over the world. No matter where we are, we look for the same things: water to swim in, grass to eat, and space to relax. As long as we have those, we know we belong.

Chapter 13: What Makes Capybara a Rodent?

Yup, I'm a rodent! That surprises a lot of people. I don't look like a mouse or a rat, but I have some very special features that prove I belong in the rodent family. Let's chew on the facts!

Rodents have two big front teeth that never stop growing, just like mine!

I use my teeth for chewing tough plants, and I have to keep nibbling to wear them down.

Rodents don't have canine teeth (like dogs or tigers), we have a big tooth gap instead.

My closest rodent cousins are guinea pigs, but I'm a LOT bigger!

Other rodents include animals like beavers, squirrels, hamsters, and porcupines.

Being a rodent means I'm great at gnawing, chewing, and surviving on plants, and I'm proud of it!

I may not look like a mouse or a squirrel, but I've got all the rodent tools: big teeth that never stop growing, a hunger for plants, and a knack for chewing just about everything. Being a rodent means I'm part of one of the toughest, cleverest animal families on Earth, and I wear that title with pride.

Chapter 14: Staying Safe in the Wild

Even though I'm peaceful, the wild can be a dangerous place! There are predators out there, so we capybaras have clever ways to stay safe, without needing claws or sharp teeth. Here's how we survive and protect each other.

Our first defense is water. We dive in and disappear fast when danger is near.

We stay close to tall grass or bushes so we can hide quickly if we need to.

One member of our herd always stays on watch, ready to alert the others with a bark.

We use our sharp hearing and sense of smell to notice predators before they get close.

When we run, we can sprint surprisingly fast, even with our short legs!

Our best trick? Staying calm. We don't panic; we move together, quietly and carefully.

The wild is full of surprises, and staying safe takes more than speed or strength, it takes calm thinking, sharp senses, and the help of your herd. I may not fight, but I know how to listen, hide, and move when it matters. In the jungle, staying peaceful is sometimes the smartest way to survive.

Chapter 15: Why Everyone Loves Capybaras!

You've probably noticed by now: I'm kind of a big deal! People around the world adore capybaras. Want to know why? It's not just because I'm cute (though that helps!). Here's why everyone calls us the friendliest animals on Earth.

I'm calm, quiet, and easy to be around. I bring peace to the animal kingdom!

I get along with almost every species: birds, monkeys, cats, dogs, even crocodiles!

I share space, take turns, and never cause trouble. No drama here!

People say I look like a potato, loaf of bread, or coconut; and they mean it as a compliment!

I've become an internet celebrity. Capybara videos go viral for being so chill and cute.

I remind people to slow down, breathe deep, and enjoy the moment. That's the capybara way.

I don't try to be famous. I just live slow, stay gentle, and make space for others. Maybe that's why people smile when they see me. In a noisy world, being quiet, kind, and calm stands out. And if my chill way of life brings peace to someone's day... well, that's the best kind of capybara magic.

Miscellaneous Facts

Capybaras can sleep with their eyes open.
This helps us stay alert even when we're resting, especially in the wild, where danger can creep up at any time.

Our name comes from the Tupi language.
The word "kapi'wara" means "grass eater" and yep, that's exactly what we do!

Capybaras can live up to 10 years in captivity.
In the wild, it's usually less—around 6 to 8 years—because life is a bit tougher without cozy naps and snack trays.

Our skin can dry out in the sun.
That's one reason we spend so much time in water and mud. It helps protect our skin from heat and bugs!

We can climb short slopes, even though we don't look like it.
Our toes spread out for extra grip, making us better walkers than you'd expect.

Some capybaras form "mega-herds."
In dry seasons, we sometimes gather in groups of over 100 capybaras near shrinking water sources!

We have scent glands on our noses and bottoms.

These help us mark territory and say, "Hey, this is my spot!" We rub on trees, rocks, or each other.

Capybara moms give birth to 2–8 pups at once.

And all the pups in the herd grow up together like one big, squeaky kindergarten class.

We don't like sudden movements or loud noises.

That's why we're so calm. Fast reactions stress us out. We prefer to observe, think, and then act.

In some places, people have called us "nature's ottomans."
Because we let birds, monkeys, and even cats sit on us. We really don't mind, as long as they're gentle!

Capybaras can hold their breath longer than most dogs.
We can stay underwater for up to 5 minutes without coming up for air!

Our babies can start eating grass within a week of birth.
Even though we drink milk, we're chewing solid food almost right away—talk about fast learners!

Our back legs are slightly longer than our front legs.

This helps us walk through tall grass and wade through muddy swamps without tipping over.

We use our noses like walkie-talkies.

Sniffing and rubbing our noses on things helps us leave behind a special scent to communicate with our herd.

Capybaras are crepuscular.

That means we're most active at dawn and dusk, when it's cool and quiet.

We don't dig burrows. We prefer open ground.
We rest in grass, mud, or shallow water, always staying near an escape route (a.k.a. the nearest pond).

Our fur dries quickly but doesn't trap warmth.
That's why we stay in warm climates. We're not built for cold weather!

Capybaras are legally classified as livestock in some countries.
In parts of South America, we're farmed just like pigs or cows, but many places also protect us now.

Our scientific name is Hydrochoerus hydrochaeris.
It means "water pig", but don't worry, we're still 100% rodent.

We can sometimes make friends with crocodiles.
In the wild, crocs rarely attack us if we're not panicking or threatening. We mind our business, they mind theirs!

Capybaras use their voices more than their faces.
We don't raise eyebrows or make big expressions, but we speak volumes with chirps, whistles, and hums.

Capybaras can jump (a little).
Not like a rabbit, but we can hop over short logs or puddles when we need to, especially as pups!

We're excellent floaters.
Our fat is evenly distributed, so we stay perfectly buoyant. Think of us as the marshmallows of the animal kingdom.

We love routine.
Same spots. Same grazing areas. Same nap times. Routine helps us feel safe and settled.

We can recognize our friends by smell.
Every capybara has a slightly different scent. We sniff each other to say "Hi, I remember you!"

Capybaras rarely fight.
If someone gets too pushy, we usually just grunt, click our teeth, or slowly walk away.

Our eyes, ears, and nose are all on top of our head.
This lets us stay mostly underwater but still see, hear, and breathe; kind of like a tiny, furry submarine!

Capybaras can run up to 35 km/h (like a human sprinter) for short bursts when scared.

Capybaras can nap with their eyes open, especially when keeping watch.

A capybara herd often has one "sentinel" that keeps watch while others nap or graze.

They're so calm that birds often build nests or perch on their backs.

Famous Capybaras

You've learned all about me, but did you know there are capybaras all over the world who've become famous? Some live in zoos, some went viral online, and some even hang out with celebrities! Let's meet some of the world's most legendary capybaras.

THE CAPYBARA ONSEN CREW
(JAPAN)

In 1996, zookeepers at Izu Shaboten Zoo noticed something surprising. When they sprayed warm water in the capybara enclosure, the animals would sit perfectly still under the stream. Soon, they tried giving them access to hot spring water (called an onsen in Japan), and the capybaras fell in love.

Every winter since, the zoo hosts daily hot spring bath sessions where capybaras soak in steamy water with floating oranges. Videos of them relaxing went viral on YouTube and TikTok, and now it's a tradition watched by millions each year. The calm expressions and closed eyes of these capys made them internet legends.

Why they're famous:
They turned into spa celebrities and helped millions discover the soothing, silly charm of capybaras.

CHEESECAKE
(THE CAPYBARA NANNY)

Cheesecake was rescued as a baby by Janice Wolf at Rocky Ridge Refuge, a sanctuary for unwanted animals. But Cheesecake didn't just grow up there—she became the caregiver for every new orphan that came in.

Goat kids, puppies, piglets, and even deer would cuddle up next to her. Cheesecake never growled or ran. She just laid quietly as animals climbed on her back or followed her around like she was their mom. Photos of her cuddling tiny dogs or sleeping in a pile of farm animals melted hearts online.

Why she's famous:
She became world-famous for being a gentle "capy-mom" to dozens of rescued animals of every shape and size.

JOEJOE THE CAPYBARA
(INSTAGRAM ROYALTY)

JoeJoe was raised by humans and became a true online celebrity. He had his own Instagram account with over 300,000 followers, where people watched videos of him getting bubble baths, wearing holiday hats, and calmly sitting in shopping carts or hammocks.

JoeJoe's calmness in unusual human situations made him endlessly shareable. Whether he was chilling in a pool or hanging out with a duck friend named Ducky, he helped the world fall in love with pet capybaras.

Why he's famous:
JoeJoe became the face of capybara cuteness, showing the internet how calm, cuddly, and curious a capybara can be.

CAPLIN ROUS
(THE PIONEER CAPYBARA)

Caplin Rous (named after the "Rodent of Unusual Size" in The Princess Bride) was one of the first capybaras to gain a loyal online following. His owner, Melanie Typaldos, used Caplin's blog and YouTube channel to educate people about capybara behavior, care, and needs.

Caplin was trained to walk on a leash, pose for photos, and even recognize commands. His content was shared by news outlets like NPR and CNN, and he became a global ambassador for capybaras.

Why he's famous:
He was the first capybara influencer, and paved the way for every internet capy after him.

DOBBY THE CAPYBARA
(AMERICA'S FAVORITE HOUSE CAPY)

Dobby lived inside a human home with baby pools, chew toys, cozy towels, and plenty of house rules! His owners shared detailed videos and blog posts showing what it's like to raise a capybara as a pet, from his picky eating habits to the sound of his purrs.

Dobby's videos were watched by millions who had never seen a capybara up close. He helped people understand both the fun and the responsibility of having such a large, social animal as a companion.

Why he's famous:
He showed the world what daily life with a house capybara really looks like, and made it impossible not to smile.

TUFF'N AND SAKURA
(THE VIRAL CAPY COUPLE)

This bonded capybara pair captured hearts across TikTok and YouTube. Their human parents share videos of Tuff'n splashing in the tub, Sakura snuggling in blankets, and both capys hanging out peacefully with dogs, rabbits, and even tortoises.

They became famous not just for their cuteness, but for showing how capybaras express affection, friendship, and personality. Fans love their differences. Tuff'n is bold, Sakura is shy.

Why they're famous:
They're a real-life capybara couple who made the internet fall in love with capy friendship and loyalty.

IPPO
(THE CAPYBARA SPA QUEEN)

Ippo became the star of Nagasaki Bio Park for one reason: she loved the hot spring more than any other capybara. When the gate opened, Ippo was always the first one to trot in and gently lower herself into the warm water, sometimes with a yuzu fruit balanced on her head!

Photos of her soaking peacefully with her eyes closed went viral every winter. Tourists from around the world came just to see Ippo's legendary bath time.

Why she's famous:
She became a symbol of calm and joy in Japan, and the face of the world's most famous capybara spa.

CHICO
(THE SUNGLASSES CAPYBARA)

Chico made headlines when college students in Brazil started posting pictures of him hanging around their campus wearing sunglasses. That's right. He would calmly sit on park benches or stroll through the grass, totally unbothered, with shades gently resting on his snout.

No one knew where Chico came from, but everyone knew he was cool. He became a local legend, with memes, fan pages, and even street art painted in his honor.

Why he's famous:
He became an urban icon for being relaxed, stylish, and completely unbothered by the busy human world.

CAPY D
(THE MEME THAT TOOK OVER THE INTERNET)

Capy D isn't just one capybara. It's the name people gave to the vibe of capybaras in internet culture. It started with a viral photo of a capybara riding on a crocodile's back, calmly floating along a muddy river. People were stunned and amused by how chill the capy looked.

From there, Capy D became the star of thousands of memes and TikTok videos, set to relaxing music. Some even made entire playlists called "capybara core" just to match the capy's calm energy.

Why he's famous:
Capy D became the ultimate symbol of peace, patience, and weird internet humor.

BUBU
(THE CAPYBARA EXPLORER)

Bubu travels the world, literally. Her human converted a camper van just for her, complete with ramps, cushions, and her own pool. Bubu has paddled in lakes in Switzerland, walked through forests in Germany, and even explored castle gardens in France.

Fans follow her travel blog and Instagram, where each new stop shows her calmly enjoying nature in different countries.

Why she's famous:
She's the most well-traveled capybara on Earth, and she's always up for a new adventure.

RIO
(THE ROOFTOP CAPYBARA)

Rio lives on the rooftop of a tall building in the middle of the city. His human built him a special green space with a small pool, sunbathing zone, and even ramps. Rio became famous on social media for videos of him relaxing with the city skyline behind him.

He became a local celebrity, known as "El Capibara de la Terraza," and people from around the world tuned in to watch this city capybara live his best life.

Why he's famous:
He showed that even in a big, noisy city, capybaras can still live calm, happy lives, if they have the right space and care.

GARIBALDI ROUS
(THE GENTLE GIANT)

Garibaldi Rous (nicknamed "Gari") was adopted after Caplin Rous passed away and carried on the mission of educating people about capybaras. He visited classrooms, appeared in interviews, and helped kids learn that capybaras are gentle, social, and need proper space and care.

Gari was known for his loving bond with his owner and for being patient during visits with children and animals alike. His passing was covered by international news.

Why he's famous:
He was a calm, kind animal ambassador who helped kids and adults understand how special capybaras really are.

Capybara vs Other Animals

People are always asking, "Cappy, are you just a giant guinea pig?" or "Are you like a beaver or a dog?" It's a fair question. I've got a big body, big teeth, and I'm super chill.

So let's find out how I really compare to other animals. You might be surprised who I'm most like!

CAPYBARA VS GUINEA PIG

Trait	Capybara	Guinea Pig

Size	Up to 150 pounds (giant!)	About 2 pounds (tiny!)
Teeth	Always growing, for chewing plants	Same. Also gnaw all day
Habitat	Rivers and wetlands	Small indoor cages or hutches
Social Life	Large herds in the wild	Pairs or small groups
Diet	Grass, fruit, water plants	Hay, veggies, pellets
Personality	Calm, gentle, quiet	Skittish, squeaky, playful

We're family! I'm just the super-sized, water-loving version.
If guinea pigs are cupcakes, I'm the full cake.

CAPYBARA VS BEAVER

Trait	Capybara 	Beaver 
Size	Up to 4 feet long and 150 pounds	3–4 feet long, up to 70 pounds
Fur	Soft, coarse, and dries quickly	Thick, waterproof, built for cold water
Habitat	Rivers, ponds, swamps, grassy wetlands	Streams, lakes, forests in North America
Social Life	Lives in large herds	Lives in small family groups
Special Skills	Great swimmer, calm and alert	Excellent builder. Makes dams and lodges
Teeth	Long front teeth for chewing plants	Powerful orange teeth for gnawing wood
Tail	No tail!	Big flat tail used for swimming and slapping the water

Beavers and I both love water, but we're built for different lives. They're the builders, I'm the drifter. Beavers build dams and shape rivers. Me? I just find a quiet spot and float. We're both calm, clever, and toothy, but I'll leave the lumber work to them!

CAPYBARA VS DOGS

Trait	Capybara	Dog

Size	Large rodent; about the size of a medium dog	Varies by breed; tiny to huge!
Temperament	Calm, quiet, peaceful	Loyal, playful, alert
Sounds	Whistles, purrs, and barks (yes, we bark too!)	Barks, whines, growls, howls
Social Life	Lives in large herds	Lives in human homes or packs
Speed	Slow and steady	Fast runners and good at chasing
Role	Wild animal or exotic pet	Domesticated pet and companion
Friendship Style	Shares space quietly	Shows affection with energy and movement

Dogs are full of energy. I'm full of chill. While they zoom around, I waddle and float. But guess what? We actually get along great! I've shared space with many dogs, and they love how peaceful I am. We're different, but that's what makes us good friends.

CAPYBARA VS RABBITS

Trait	Capybara 	Rabbit 
Size	Very large; up to 150 pounds	Small; usually 2–6 pounds
Body Type	Round and heavy, built for swimming	Small and light, built for hopping
Habitat	Rivers, swamps, grassy wetlands	Meadows, forests, underground burrows
Movement	Walks and swims slowly	Hops and sprints quickly
Teeth	Long front teeth for chewing plants	Also has ever-growing teeth
Social Life	Lives in herds	Some live alone, others in groups
Sounds	Whistles, barks, purrs	Soft thumps, squeaks, gentle growls

Rabbits and I both love plants, soft ground, and a peaceful life, but they bounce while I float! They're quick and twitchy. I'm slow and steady. We both know how to stay quiet and cozy, and we both know how to keep those teeth in check!

Capybara Communication Guide

We capybaras may not speak with words, but we're great communicators! We use different sounds to tell our family how we feel; whether we're happy, scared, playful, or just saying "Hi, I'm here!" Let me teach you a few of our favorite capy-language sounds.

Purr

Sound: Mmmrrrrr

This soft, humming sound means I'm feeling cozy and calm, usually when I'm relaxing, getting groomed, or cuddling with my herd.

Whistle

Sound: Peeeeep

This high-pitched noise means I'm excited or calling out to my friends. Baby capys whistle when they want attention or when they're looking for Mom!

Bark

Sound: ARK!

This sharp, sudden sound means danger! I bark to warn my group when I sense something suspicious. It's loud, fast, and gets everyone moving.

Click or Chatter

Sound: Ch-ch-ch-ch

When I'm annoyed or warning others to give me space, I click my teeth or chatter softly. It's like saying, "Hey, back off a little."

Squeal

Sound: Eeeek!

This usually means I'm uncomfortable, upset, or nervous. Baby capys might squeal if they get separated from their group.

Tooth Grinding

Sound: Low scraping noise

This isn't angry, it usually means I'm sleepy or content. Kind of like humans humming while they rest.

And just like that... our capy adventure has come to an end! Thanks for splashing, snacking, and sunbathing with me. I loved showing you around my world.

Now that you know all about capybaras, I hope you'll keep exploring, learning, and being kind to animals, nature, and yourself.

Remember: stay calm, stay curious, and stay capy-cool.

Until next time...
Your friend,
Cappy 🐾

CERTIFICATE OF CAPYBARA EXPERTISE!

This certifies that

____

has officially completed the journey through the world of capybaras and now knows how to eat, nap, float, chew, and chill like a true capybara champion!

Presented by: Cappy the Capybara

on ____________________